ISAAC ASIMOV'S NEW LIBRARY OF THE UNIVERSE

EXPLORING OUTER SPACE:
ROCKETS, PROBES, AND SATELLITES

BY ISAAC ASIMOV

WITH REVISIONS AND UPDATING BY FRANCIS REDDY

Gareth Stevens Publishing

MILWAUKEE

For a free color catalog describing Gareth Stevens' list of high-quality books, call 1-800-542-2595 (USA) or 1-800-461-9120 (Canada). Gareth Stevens' Fax: (414) 225-0377.

Library of Congress Cataloging-in-Publication Data

Asimov, Isaac.
  Exploring outer space: rockets, probes, and satellites / by Isaac Asimov ; with revisions and updating by Francis Reddy.
    p. cm. — (Isaac Asimov's new library of the universe)
  Rev. ed. of: Rockets, probes, and satellites. 1988.
  Includes bibliographical references and index.
  ISBN 0-8368-1193-3
  1. Rocketry--Juvenile literature. 2. Artificial satellites--Juvenile literature. 3. Space probes--Juvenile literature. [1. Rocketry. 2. Artificial satellites. 3. Space probes.] I. Reddy, Francis, 1959- . II. Asimov, Isaac. Rockets, probes, and satellites. III. Title. IV. Series: Asimov, Isaac. New library of the universe.
  TL793.A825 1995
  629.43'5--dc20   94-31254

This edition first published in 1995 by
Gareth Stevens Publishing
1555 North RiverCenter Drive, Suite 201
Milwaukee, Wisconsin 53212, USA

Project editor: Barbara J. Behm
Design adaptation: Helene Feider
Editorial assistant: Diane Laska
Production director: Susan Ashley
Picture research: Kathy Keller
Artwork commissioning: Kathy Keller and Laurie Shock

Printed in the United States of America

1 2 3 4 5 6 7 8 9 99 98 97 96 95

To bring this classic of young people's information up to date, the editors at Gareth Stevens Publishing have selected two noted science authors, Greg Walz-Chojnacki and Francis Reddy. Walz-Chojnacki and Reddy coauthored the recent book *Celestial Delights: The Best Astronomical Events Through 2001.*

Walz-Chojnacki is also the author of the book *Comet: The Story Behind Halley's Comet* and various articles about the space program. He was an editor of *Odyssey,* an astronomy and space technology magazine for young people, for eleven years.

Reddy is the author of nine books, including *Halley's Comet, Children's Atlas of the Universe, Children's Atlas of Earth Through Time,* and *Children's Atlas of Native Americans,* plus numerous articles. He was an editor of *Astronomy* magazine for several years.

CONTENTS

We live in an enormously large place – the Universe. It's just in the last fifty-five years or so that we've found out how large it probably is. It's only natural that we would want to understand the place in which we live, so scientists have developed instruments – such as radio telescopes, satellites, probes, and many more – that have told us far more about the Universe than could possibly be imagined.

We have seen planets up close. We have learned about quasars and pulsars, black holes, and supernovas. We have gathered amazing data about how the Universe may have come into being and how it may end. Nothing could be more astonishing.

One of the ways we have discovered the Universe is through the use of rockets. With rockets, we have been able to send probes to distant planets, and put artificial satellites into orbit around Earth. We have sent astronauts into space, and some of them have even walked on the Moon. Rockets, probes, and satellites have all contributed a great deal to unraveling the mystery of our vast Universe.

Isaac Asimov

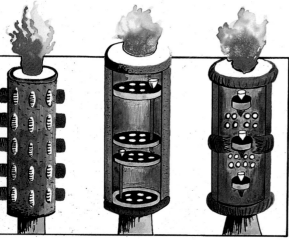

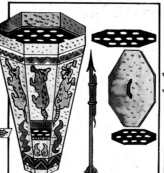

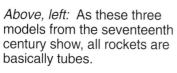

Above, left: As these three models from the seventeenth century show, all rockets are basically tubes.

Above, center: The pieces of a seventeenth-century Chinese rocket arrow launcher are shown. Each hole in the launcher held a rocket, and all rockets could be fired at once.

Above, right: This is a drawing of an arsenal of rockets used during the thirteenth century by Mongolians in wars against Japan, the Middle East, and Europe.

Rockets' Red Glare

The fascinating invention known as the rocket came about in a country that now has the world's fourth largest space program after the United States, Russia, and the European Space Agency.

It was in China, in the 1200s, that people first packed gunpowder into a cardboard cylinder. When the gunpowder was lit by a fuse, gases were formed that pushed backward, moving the rocket forward. In 1687, an English scientist, Sir Isaac Newton, explained the science of how the rocket moved forward when the gunpowder exploded. His explanation is known as the law of action and reaction.

In the early 1800s, rockets were sometimes used to carry explosives used in warfare. Francis Scott Key wrote about this in the national anthem of the United States, "The Star Spangled Banner," with the words *the rockets' red glare*.

Top: A rocket shows Newton's law of action and reaction.
(Upper) Liquid hydrogen and oxygen are sent to the combustion chamber, where they mix and ignite.
(Lower) The hot gases created by the ignition rush out of the nozzle (the action), causing the rocket to move in the opposite direction (the reaction).

Left: A rocket launches a Chinese communications satellite into orbit.

5

The Early Days of Rocketry

By the early twentieth century, some scientists had begun to realize that rockets were one way that objects could be sent into space. The first scientist to understand this, beginning in 1903, was a Russian, Konstantin Eduardovich Tsiolkovsky. An American, Robert H. Goddard, continued that work. In 1926, Goddard launched the first rocket using gasoline and liquid oxygen instead of gunpowder. For the next fifteen years, Goddard kept designing and launching better and better rockets. Unfortunately, rockets big and powerful enough to use in space also meant that some people would want to use them to carry weapons of war right here on Earth.

Below, left: In the early 1900s, Konstantin Eduardovich Tsiolkovsky suggested ideas about rocketry that have since become a reality. His suggestions included using liquid oxygen and hydrogen to fuel high-speed rockets and using artificial satellites and jet-propelled rockets in space. Robert H. Goddard carried on this work.

Below, right: Goddard with the world's first liquid-fueled rocket in 1926. This picture was probably taken in Goddard's backyard, where he usually launched his rockets.

Right: Goddard at Clark University in Worcester, Massachusetts, in 1924.

Moon

mit of balloon; 20 miles

limit of atmosphere;
200 miles

700 miles

-6 miles/s   c 2

1 lb

sol's (H)

The Space Age Begins

During World War II, the Germans developed rockets big enough and powerful enough to bomb London, England. After the war, both the United States and the former Soviet Union began to develop large rockets for exploring space.

On October 4, 1957, a Soviet rocket launched Earth's first artificial satellite. The satellite was called *Sputnik 1*. *Sputnik 1* circled Earth in an egg-shaped orbit 142-588 miles (228-947 kilometers) high every ninety minutes.

Shortly thereafter, on January 31, 1958, the United States launched a satellite, *Explorer 1*. The Space Age had begun!

Opposite: The ugly aftermath of the German bombing of London during World War II, when rockets were used.

Top: On October 4, 1957, *Sputnik 1* blasted off from the former Soviet Union and began to orbit Earth. It weighed 184 pounds (83 kilograms).

Bottom: In the Russian language, *sputnik* means "traveling companion." On November 3, 1957, *Sputnik 2* became Earth's second artificial satellite. It carried a dog named Laika, the first living being in space.

! ***Catch some satellite-shine!***

Some artificial satellites are visible from Earth. They look like bright stars moving slowly across the night sky. They can be seen best just after sunset or just before dawn, when the satellite is in daylight but the sky is still dark where you are. We can see satellites because they reflect sunlight – just like our own natural satellite, the Moon.

9

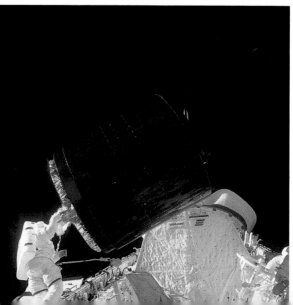

Opposite, top: In 1993, astronauts aboard the U.S. space shuttle *Endeavour* performed a series of demanding space walks to fix the Hubble SpaceTelescope. Astronaut Kathryn C. Thornton refers to a notebook on her arm to make repairs to the telescope.

Opposite, bottom, left: A Canadian communications satellite just seconds after lift-off.

Opposite, bottom, center: U.S. astronauts Joe Allen and Dale Gardner move a stranded communications satellite into *Discovery*'s cargo bay for its trip back to Earth in 1984.

Opposite, bottom, right: U.S. astronaut Joe Allen as he helps rescue another stranded satellite.

Below, left: The image of astronaut F. Story Musgrave is reflected in the Hubble Space Telescope high above Earth. Musgrave made repairs to the telescope in 1993.

Below, right: Astronaut Jeffrey A. Hoffman joins Musgrave to install a new camera on the Hubble Space Telescope.

Working in Space

While satellites circle Earth, they do many kinds of work. For example, communications satellites receive radio waves from one place, make them stronger, and send them to a completely different place. Today, thanks to satellites, television programs and telephone calls can be sent easily from continent to continent. And since 1981, space shuttles have carried satellites into space and placed them in orbit.

Predicting Weather Conditions

Weather satellites began to be launched into space in 1960. These satellites orbit Earth, taking photographs of our planet and transmitting them back to Earth in the form of radio waves. The radio waves are used by meteorologists to create the weather-related pictures shown on television. The pictures show the movement of clouds above Earth. Observing this movement allows meteorologists to predict the weather. This is especially important when dangerous weather is approaching. For example, before 1960, meteorologists couldn't always tell when a hurricane might strike. But thanks to weather satellites, people can now receive fair warning of dangerous weather and take precautions.

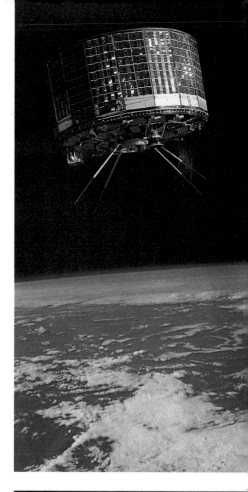

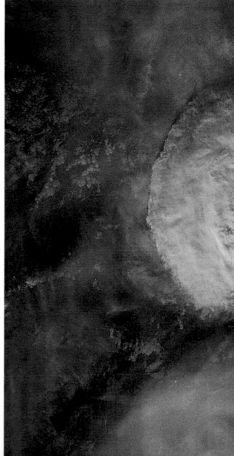

Top: Tiros 8 is a weather satellite sent into orbit in 1963 to take pictures of cloud patterns and instantly transmit them to Earth.

Opposite, top: A thermal (heat) map of Florida and Cuba taken by the *Nimbus 5* weather satellite. As indicated by the various colors, Cuba and the water along the Gulf Coast (in red) are warmer than Florida and Mexico's Yucatán Peninsula (in blue and green). In Florida, Lake Okeechobee (in yellow) and the Everglades (in red) are warmer than other parts of Florida.

Bottom, center: Thunderclouds over the Amazon Basin, Brazil. *Apollo 9* took the photograph.

Opposite, bottom: A dramatic Earth-sky shot of Hurricane Gladys (1968) as seen from the *Apollo 7* spacecraft, 99 miles (160 km) above the Gulf of Mexico.

Below: A map containing information sent back to Earth by *Nimbus 7* shows the ozone layer that protects Earth from some of the Sun's ultraviolet rays. The dark violet area shows a deep hole in the ozone over Antarctica. This hole was created by chemicals that the modern world has released into the atmosphere.

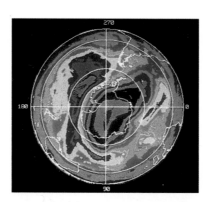

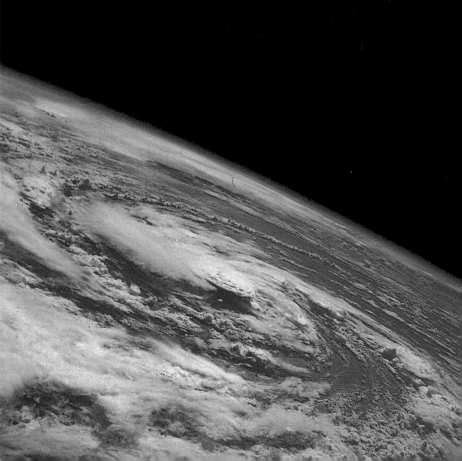

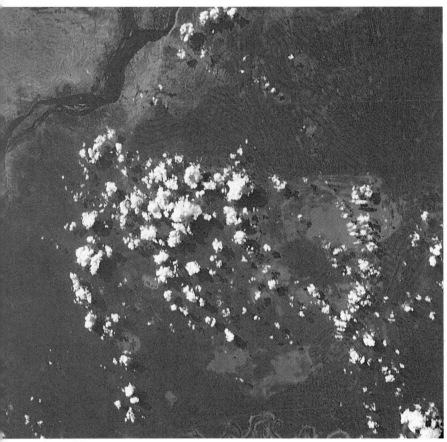

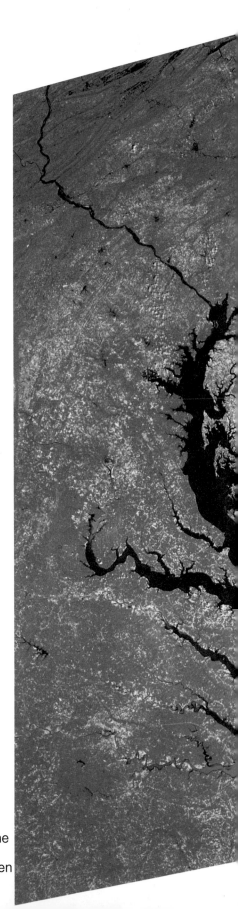

Top, left: High above Florida, the space shuttle *Challenger*, atop its plume of steam, heads toward outer space on its second mission (1983).

Top, right: This satellite picture shows Italy's "boot," other parts of Europe, and North Africa.

Above: A satellite view of the Arizona-Utah border area showing the Colorado River and the Grand Canyon.

Right: The eastern coast of the United States from New York City to Norfolk, Virginia, as seen by satellite.

Studying Earth by Satellite

When clouds aren't in the way, satellites can take pictures of Earth itself. This makes it possible to have very exact maps of Earth.

Satellite pictures can also reveal the condition of forests and croplands, pinpointing trouble situations such as the spread of plant diseases. The ocean and its schools of fish can be studied by satellite. A ship can receive messages from satellites to find its exact position in the sea.

Many satellites do this work from what is known as a geostationary orbit. They stay over one area of Earth at all times. A geostationary satellite must be at least 22,170 miles (35,680 km) high. A satellite at this height can orbit at the same speed as Earth's rotation. This allows it to stay in one place above Earth. Geostationary satellites may be used for telecommunications, weather forecasting, and even spying.

! The ups and downs of spying by satellite

A spy satellite might take a picture of Earth from 100 miles (160 km) up. This picture is so clear that you can tell if a coin on the ground is heads or tails! Some spy satellites are positioned even higher. In 1987, a U.S. geostationary spy satellite located over Lebanon spotted a group of hostages being moved from one building to another. The satellite's recorders and cameras taped walkie-talkie conversations, revealed the faces of some of the hostages, and determined what materials the buildings were made of. All this could be accomplished at night or through thick clouds from a height of at least 22,170 miles (35,680 km)! It is incredible to think about spy satellites and the amazing things they can see – and even hear – from outer space.

Worlds Beyond

Satellites orbit Earth and can tell us about other worlds, as well as our own. Space probes can take us close to these other worlds and even land on them. The nearest world beyond Earth is the Moon. It is about 240,000 miles (386,000 km) away. The first probe raced past the Moon in 1959 and returned pictures of its far side, the side that is always turned away from Earth. Seven years later, probes landed on the Moon and returned pictures from the Moon's surface. Finally, on July 20, 1969, a piloted spacecraft touched down on the Moon. U.S. astronaut Neil Armstrong became the first person to step onto another world.

Top: Apollo 11 commander Neil Armstrong in his lunar module (July 1969) on the Moon.

Center: A view of the surface of the near side of the Moon from *Apollo 8.* The large crater is about 20 miles (32 km) across.

Bottom: A view of the far side of the Moon.

Opposite, top: An artist's rendition of an assortment of satellites and probes leaving home base, Earth, behind. *Clockwise, from upper right: Voyager* (U.S.), *Mariner 6* or *7* (U.S.), *Ulysses* (European Space Agency), *Pioneer* (U.S.), Hubble Space Telescope (U.S.), *Vega* (former Soviet Union), and *Galileo* (U.S.).

Opposite, bottom: In 1969, *Apollo 12* astronaut Pete Conrad poses with *Surveyor 3,* a robot lander that arrived on the Moon two and a half years earlier. Information from the *Surveyor* probes helped pave the way for human landings on the Moon.

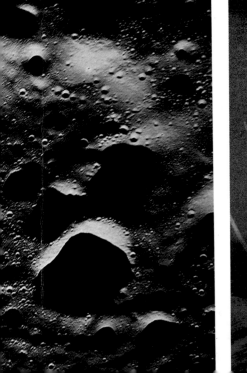

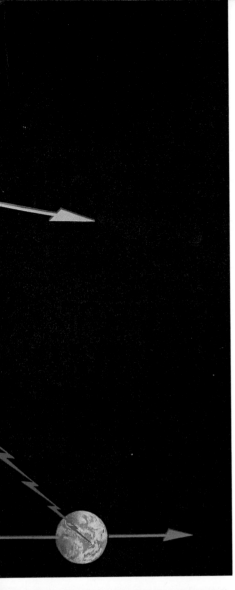

Probing Mercury

No human being has yet gone farther than the Moon, but unpiloted probes have. In 1974 and 1975, a probe called *Mariner 10* (U.S.) skimmed by the planet Mercury several times. It came within 203 miles (327 km) of the surface, taking photographs as it went by. Mercury is the planet that is closest to the Sun. Before *Mariner 10*, Mercury was seen only as a tiny circle. The probe showed most of Mercury's surface in full detail. It looks very much like our Moon, with many craters on its surface.

Top: This image illustrates *Mariner 10* swooping past the sunlit side of Mercury and transmitting pictures back to Earth.

Opposite, bottom: With no atmosphere to burn up striking asteroids, tiny Mercury has taken quite a beating in its billions of years in the Solar System.

Left: Moonlike Mercury is the smallest of the rocky planets and the second smallest planet (after Pluto) in the Solar System. *Mariner 10* has given us our only close-up views of Mercury so far. This photo was pieced together from many images taken by *Mariner 10* from a distance of 124,000 miles (200,000 km) above the planet.

Unveiling Venus

The first space probes flew past Venus in 1962. They showed that its dense atmosphere held in heat, making Venus even hotter than sun-baked Mercury. They also showed that the surface of Venus was always hidden beneath thick clouds. Landers sent back pictures of the surface before being destroyed by the intense heat.

Until more recent times, a global view of the planet remained concealed behind a cloudy veil. But radio waves can penetrate clouds. Radio telescopes on Earth made the first crude maps of Venus. In the 1970s and 1980s, probes from the U.S. and the former Soviet Union orbited Venus and provided even better maps. The U.S. *Magellan* probe has supplied the clearest pictures of Venus. It mapped 99 percent of the planet's surface by radar from 1990 to 1994. *Magellan* has returned more data than all other U.S. planetary probes combined.

! *Probing the Venusian cloud cover*

Venus is almost the same size as Earth, but it is a little closer to the Sun. Clouds covering · its surface are made of water and sulfuric acid. It was once thought that Venus might contain life. However, probes have shown that Venus is extremely hot and, as a result, dry. Venus turns very slowly. It makes only one turn in 243 days, and it turns in a different direction than most planets. Earth and almost all the worlds in the Solar System turn from west to east. Venus turns from east to west.

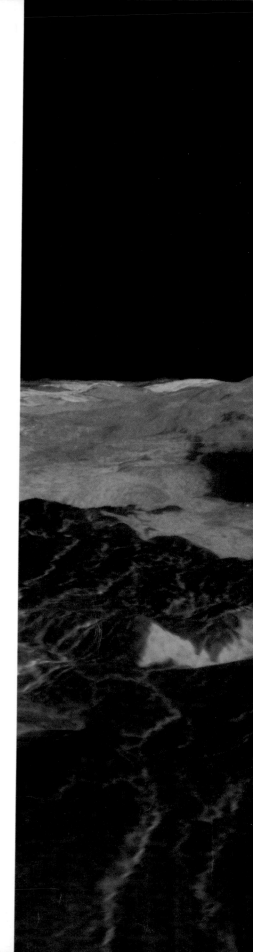

Right: Maat Mons, a volcano 3 miles (5 km) high on Venus, looms in the distance. Bright areas trace ancient lava flows, some of which partially cover the crater Melba, which is 14 miles (23 km) across.

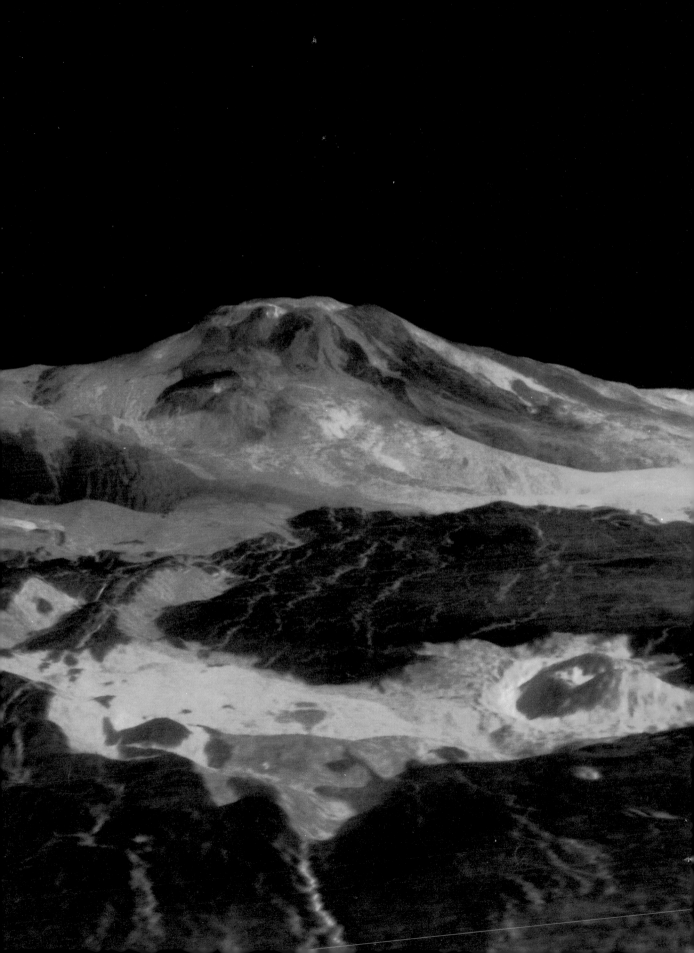

Is There Life on Mars?

Could there be life on Mars? We now know how to answer this question better than ever before. During the early 1900s, some astronomers thought they saw thin, straight lines, called canals, on the surface of Mars. They thought intelligent beings might exist there. Beginning in 1965, Mars probes passed by the planet and sent back photographs. The photographs showed there are no canals. There are, instead, canyons, dead volcanoes, numerous craters, and a very thin atmosphere. In 1976, two probes, *Viking 1* and *Viking 2*, landed on Martian soil. These probes tested the soil to see if simple life, as we know it, might exist on Mars. It seems that none does.

❓ *Probing Mars – many questions remain*

There are no canals on Mars, but there are markings on its surface that look like dried-up rivers. Could it be that some time long ago there was water on Mars? If so, what happened to it? And during the time when there might have been water on Mars, did life develop? If so, are there any traces of life left? Mars is the planet most like Earth, and anything we can do to understand it further might help us understand our planet Earth more, too.

Top: This photo of the Martian landscape was taken shortly before sunset by the *Viking 1* lander. Part of the lander is visible in the photo.

Opposite, bottom: These two sets of photos were made from images taken by the *Viking* probes. *(Top)* This picture shows a section of the northern polar ice cap on Mars where wind may have driven bits of ice and soil into a streaked pattern. *(Bottom)* The Martian landscape has smooth areas and craters.

Left: Pictured is a full-size working model of the *Viking* lander. It is 7 feet (2.1 m) high and weighs about a ton. Its special features include a soil sampler (extended in front) and two camera "eyes" that stick up just behind the sampler.

Top: Leaving first Jupiter, then Saturn, Uranus, and Neptune behind, *Voyager 2* heads for the stars.

Center, left: *Voyager 1* took this spectacular picture of Io, one of Jupiter's large moons. A huge volcanic explosion appears just over Io's horizon.

Center, right: *Voyager 2* photographed Saturn and its magnificent rings from a distance of about 2.1 million miles (3.4 million km) away.

Bottom, left: An audio recording was carried aboard *Voyager 2*. Its material is geared to any extraterrestrials who care to listen and includes music and a greeting from former U.S. President Jimmy Carter.

Bottom, right: *Voyager 1* clearly shows the flat, solid-ice surface of Europa, a moon of Jupiter.

Journeying to Jupiter and Beyond

Several probes with the names *Pioneer* and *Voyager* have gone to the farthest reaches of our Solar System. Beginning in 1973, they started to explore the giant planets that circle the Sun at great distances. They skimmed by Jupiter, the largest, and studied its natural satellites, or moons. They found live volcanoes on one moon, Io, and a worldwide glacier on another moon, Europa. Beyond Jupiter, they sent back close-up pictures of Saturn and its enormous rings. In 1989, rings around Neptune and ice volcanoes on its moon Triton were discovered by probes.

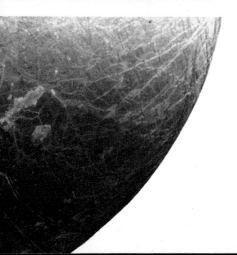

! *Probing Jupiter, a giant among giants*

Jupiter is the largest of the planets. It is 318 times as massive as Earth. It has more than twice the mass of all the other planets put together. It also has many natural satellites, or moons. Four of them are quite large. One moon, Ganymede, is the largest of all the moons in the Solar System. In fact, it is actually larger than the planet Mercury! Jupiter's next largest satellite is Callisto. Both Callisto and Ganymede are made up largely of ice and are covered with craters. Jupiter also has a thin ring around it that was first discovered by probes, but it is tiny compared to the enormous rings of Saturn.

25

Above: The day will come when space shuttles will routinely carry astronauts and equipment to and from space stations like the one pictured. These stations would give us a base for observing the cosmos and for sending probes and people to other parts of the Solar System.

A Future of Discovery

Satellites and space probes will help us continue our exploration of the Solar System and beyond. For instance, astronauts successfully repaired the Hubble Space Telescope in 1993, clearing its vision of deep space. The Compton Gamma Ray Observatory is collecting data on the most powerful processes in the Universe. A new generation of weather satellites has begun monitoring our weather. In 1994, the Shuttle Imaging Radar took a look at Earth the way *Magellan* looked at Venus. Data from this mission and others will help scientists study changes in the global environment.

The *Galileo* mission to Jupiter is now exploring the many moons of the Solar System's largest planet. In a few years, the *Cassini* mission to Saturn will improve our knowledge of the ringed planet and its moons. *Voyager 1* and *2* and *Pioneer 10* and *11* are our most distant probes. They will, one day, leave our Solar System altogether and head toward distant worlds. Scientists hope they'll continue returning information to Earth for decades.

? *Discovering Saturn's moon, Titan*

Saturn has a moon that is almost as large as Jupiter's moon, Ganymede. It is Titan, the second largest natural satellite in the Solar System. Since Titan is nearly twice as far from the Sun as Ganymede, it is much colder there than on Ganymede. A cold world holds an atmosphere better than a warm one. Titan has the thickest atmosphere of any known moon in our Solar System – even thicker than on Neptune's large moon, Triton. But Titan's atmosphere is also misty, and scientists cannot see its surface. What is Titan like beneath its atmosphere? It is not yet known.

Fact File: A Sky Filled with Satellites

The nations of Earth have launched an incredible assortment of satellites into space. These satellites give us new ways of understanding our Earth and outer space, predicting the weather, communicating with one another, performing technological experiments, and even spying on one another.

Although dozens of countries have launched satellites into space, few of these nations have their own launch sites. Therefore, many countries must use the launch pads of other countries. The chart below gives information about some major launch sites, along with clues to help locate the sites on a map. Most countries try to build their launch sites close to the Equator, which is at 0° latitude. This is because the Earth spins eastward with greater velocity, or speed, closer to the Equator. So a rocket launched near the Equator would get a greater natural boost into space from the planet's rotation.

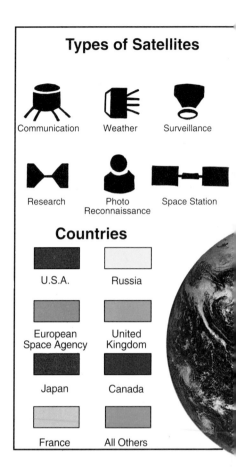

Some of the World's Major Launch Sites

Country:	U.S.A.	RUSSIAN FEDERATION	EUROPEAN SPACE AGENCY
Site	Kennedy Space Center	Tyuratam-Baikonur	Kourou
Location	Cape Canaveral, Florida	Kazakhstan	French Guiana
Latitude & Longitude	28.5° north 81° west	46° north 63.5° east	5.3° north 52.5° west
Comments*	Chief U.S. site. Called Cape Kennedy 1963-1973, then renamed Canaveral.	All piloted Russian craft launched here.	The major space center for European Space Agency (ESA) program.

* "Comments" from information in *Quest for Space* by Luigi Broglio, et al. (New York: Crescent Books, 1987).

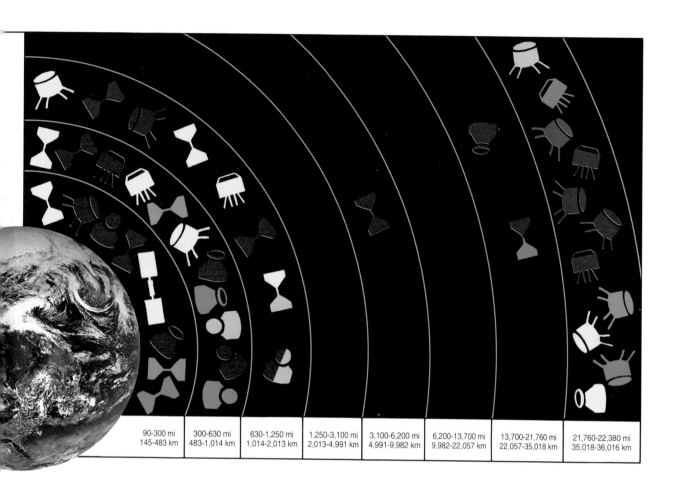

| 90-300 mi | 300-630 mi | 630-1,250 mi | 1,250-3,100 mi | 3,100-6,200 mi | 6,200-13,700 mi | 13,700-21,760 mi | 21,760-22,380 mi |
| 145-483 km | 483-1,014 km | 1,014-2,013 km | 2,013-4,991 km | 4,991-9,982 km | 9,982-22,057 km | 22,057-35,018 km | 35,018-36,016 km |

ITALY	**JAPAN**	**CHINA**	**INDIA**
San Marco	Kagoshima-Uchinoura	Shuang-ch'eng-tzu ("East Wind")	SHAR-Sriharikota
Formosa (Ungama) Bay, Kenya	Kyushu Island, Japan	Jiayuguan, China	Sriharikota Island, India
2.9° south 41° east	31° north 130.4° east	40.25° north 99.5° east	13.5° north 81.3° east
Launch site of U.S. Uhuru satellite — first discovery of a black hole.	Built for launch of University of Tokyo scientific satellites only.	Run by team of technicians trained in both U.S. and Russia.	First launching in 1971. Also one of four Indian space study centers.

Index

Born in 1920, Isaac Asimov came to the United States as a young boy from his native Russia. As a young man, he was a student of biochemistry. In time, he became one of the most productive writers the world has ever known. His books cover a spectrum of topics, including science, history, language theory, fantasy, and science fiction. His brilliant imagination gained him the respect and admiration of adults and children alike. Sadly, Isaac Asimov died shortly after the publication of the first edition of *Isaac Asimov's Library of the Universe.*

The publishers wish to thank the following for permission to reproduce copyright material: front cover, NASA; 4 (all), © Laurie Shock 1988; 4-5 (upper), © Sally Bensusen 1987; 4-5 (lower), Xin Hua News Agency; 6 (left), Oberg Archives; 6 (right), NASA; 6-7, Smithsonian Institution; 8, Imperial War Museum; 9 (upper), Oberg Archives; 9 (lower), Smithsonian Institution; 10-11 (all), 12-13 (all), 14 (upper left and lower), NASA; 14 (upper right), European Space Agency; 14-15, 16 (both), 16-17, NASA; 17 (upper), © Lynette Cook/Morrison Planetarium 1987; 17 (lower), 18-19 (all), NASA; 20-21, Jet Propulsion Laboratory; 22-23 (all), 24 (both), NASA; 24-25 (upper), © Julian Baum 1987; 24-25 (lower), National Space Science Data Center; 25, NASA; 26-27, Johnson Space Center/NASA; 28-29 (inset), NASA; 28-29 (large), © Kathy Keller and Laurie Shock.